CAN'T I JUST
STAY IN MY ROOM?
A Career Guide for Everyone
Who'd Rather Not Talk About It

Jennifer Larsen

Originality Statement

This book is an original work written by the author and reflects their unique ideas, voice, and instructional approach. While it may reference common educational and career-planning concepts, all content, including structure, language, exercises, and framework, is the author's own creation. Any similarities to other published works are purely coincidental.

Printed in the United States of America

First Edition

Cover design by Rachel Bostwick

Interior design and layout by Rachel Bostwick

Contents

📖 Introduction: Finding Your Path—Without Wasting Time or Money

◆ The Big Question: What Do You Want to Do with Your Life?

At some point, everyone gets asked:

"What do you want to do with your life?"

It sounds simple, but for most people, it's **overwhelming.** Whether you're just starting out or trying to figure things out for the **fifth time**, the pressure to **"get it right"** can feel huge.

And it's not just you—**parents struggle with this too.** They want the best for their kids, and when they don't know what to say, they often **default to pushing financial security.** It's understandable—nobody wants their child to struggle. But this has led to a frustrating trend:

◆ The Two Biggest Career Pitfalls:

> ✗ Some students pick a degree they enjoy but **have no idea how to turn it into a career.**

> ✗ Others choose a major **just because it pays well**, even if they **hate the work.**

Neither path leads to happiness. **No one should spend 50 years in a job they can't stand.** And no one should go **$100,000 into debt** for a degree they can't apply.

☑ The good news? There's a better way.

◆ **You Don't Have to Have It All Figured Out Yet**

Many people believe that they need to **know exactly what they want to do before making any decisions.**

🚫 **Wrong.**

✓ **College is part of the journey, not the final destination.** You can use those years to **explore interests and build skills** instead of feeling pressured to choose the perfect major right away.

✓ **College isn't the only option.** Some of the highest-paying and most in-demand careers **don't require a degree at all.**

✓ **Your first career decision isn't permanent.** Most people **change paths multiple times** as they discover what truly fits.

This book isn't here to tell you, **"Pick a major and stick with it forever."** Instead, it will show you **how to make informed decisions, test out careers, and adjust your path as you go.**

✅ **Key Takeaway:** You don't have to know **everything** today—you just need to **start moving forward.**

♦ **A Career That Actually Fits You—Not Just a "Safe" Option**

This book will help you figure out a **career path that makes sense for you**—not just something that **pays the bills,** and not just something you **enjoy for fun,** but a **real, sustainable future that balances both.**

To do that, you only need to focus on **three things:**

1 **What are you good at?** (Even the skills you don't realize matter.)

2 **What do you like?** (Because passion does count.)

3 **What does society need?** (A job has to be sustainable, too.)

When you combine these three, you'll start seeing real options—careers that fit **who you are, what you enjoy, and what will actually support you.**

And once you have that foundation, making decisions about **college, trade school, bootcamps, military service, or job choices** becomes **much easier.**

◆ **College: A Good Option—But Not the Only One**

For years, people were told that **college was the only path to success.**

🚫 **That's simply not true.**

✓ Some of the **most in-demand careers don't require a degree.**

✓ You can build **marketable skills** through **trade schools, bootcamps, self-teaching, or apprenticeships.**

✓ If you **do** choose college, you don't have to **pick a major right away, and you can adjust as you go.**

If you're unsure about college, **this book will help you explore all of your options.**

◆ The Reality: Your Career Will Evolve—And That's Okay

Another **huge myth** about career planning is that you need to **figure it all out now** and stick with it for life.

✓ Most people change careers multiple times.

✓ Industries shift, technology evolves, and new jobs appear all the time.

✓ The "perfect" career today might not even exist in 10 years.

That's why this book **doesn't just help you choose a career—it also prepares you for change.**

If you **realize you want to switch paths later,** there are ways to do it **without starting over from scratch.** If the **job market changes,** you'll know how to **adapt and keep your career moving forward.**

Key Takeaway: Your first career choice **isn't your final one.** The most valuable skill you can develop is **learning how to navigate change.**

◆ What You'll Learn in This Book

This isn't a long, complicated book full of **fluff and outdated career advice**. It's a **straight-to-the-point guide** to help you **find direction and move forward with confidence.**

◆ By the end, you'll know how to:

✓ **Identify your real skills** (including the ones you don't even realize are valuable).

✓ **Uncover what you actually enjoy doing**—beyond just hobbies.

✓ **Research the job market** so you don't waste time on careers that are disappearing.

✓ **Choose a college major strategically—or decide if college is even the right path.**

✓ **Explore alternatives like trade school, bootcamps, the military, or entrepreneurship.**

✓ **Test out careers before committing** (so you don't waste years on something you'll regret).

✓ **Make a career plan—but also pivot if you ever change your mind.**

✓ **Future-proof your career** so you always stay ahead of industry shifts.

◆ And most importantly:

✓ **Take action.** Because all the career advice in the world means nothing if you don't apply it.

By the end, **you'll have a plan.** You won't be guessing. You won't feel lost. **And if you still need help, you'll know exactly where to find it.**

◆ **What Happens Next?**

✓ If you're **stressed about choosing a career,** this book will help you break it down into **simple, manageable steps.**

✓ If you **already have a career plan,** this book will show you how to **test it before committing.**

✓ If you're **afraid of picking the wrong path,** this book will teach you how to **pivot later if needed.**

Your **career is yours to shape.** Let's get started. 🚀

📖 Chapter 1: What Are You Good At?

Skills Aren't Always Obvious

Most people think of skills in big, obvious ways—math, writing, sports, science. But the skills that truly shape careers often go unnoticed.

Think about it:

- ✔ Some people can sit in front of a computer for hours without getting distracted. That's a skill.

- ✔ Some are great at organizing, keeping everything in order effortlessly.

- ✔ Some instinctively know which colors match or how to arrange a space to make it feel balanced.

These don't sound like job qualifications, but they absolutely are. **The problem is, most people don't realize their own strengths because no one ever points them out.**

◆ **Breaking Past the Obvious Skills**

When someone asks, **"What are you good at?"** the typical responses are:

      ✖ "I don't know."

      ✖ "I guess I'm okay at math."

      ✖ "I like video games, but that's not a skill."

But let's dig deeper. Here are some hidden skills that people often overlook:

☑ Do you remember details well (like dates, facts, or instructions)?
→ That's a skill.

☑ Do you pick up on other people's moods easily?
→ Emotional intelligence is a skill.

☑ Do you enjoy solving puzzles, fixing things, or figuring out how something works?
→ Critical thinking is a skill.

☑ Do you find it easy to explain things to others?
→ That's a teaching or communication skill.

◆ The Difference Between Skills and Talents

A *skill* is something you can **learn and improve** over time.

A *talent* is something you're naturally inclined to be good at.

For example:

• **Skill:** You learn how to code by practicing.

• **Talent:** You naturally understand patterns and logic, making it easier for you to grasp coding concepts quickly.

Why does this matter? **Because even if you don't feel naturally talented in something, skills can always be developed.**

◆ Example:

Let's say you're not great at public speaking. That doesn't mean you're doomed to struggle with communication forever. If you practice, take a course, and gain experience, you can **develop that skill** and become excellent at it—even if it never felt "natural" to you.

Key Takeaway: If you assume you're only allowed to pursue careers based on natural talent, you'll **severely limit your options**.

◆ **Expanding Your View of Skills**

Sometimes, the skills that seem small actually open **huge career opportunities**.

   ✓ **Example 1: The "Social Butterfly" Skill**

- You might think, "I just like talking to people."

- But this skill applies to careers like **sales, public relations, customer service, HR, coaching, or event planning**.

   ✓ **Example 2: The "Always Fixing Things" Skill**

- If you're always fixing things around the house or tinkering with gadgets, that's a **problem-solving skill**.

- This can lead to careers in **engineering, IT, mechanics, cybersecurity, or even entrepreneurship**.

   ✓ **Example 3: The "Creative Organizer" Skill**

- If you love organizing but also enjoy aesthetics, you might be great at **event planning, interior design, project management, or even social media marketing**.

- **Why Your "Weird" Skills Matter**

Think of skills as puzzle pieces. Even the small, quirky ones fit somewhere. You just need to figure out how they connect.

Example: A person who loves video games might assume that's useless in the job world. But if they break it down into skills, they might realize:

- **Strategic thinking** → Great for **marketing, business analysis, or management**.

- **Hand-eye coordination** → Useful in **surgery, robotics, and animation**.

- **Fast decision-making** → Needed in **law enforcement, finance, and emergency response careers**.

Key Takeaway: Just because a skill doesn't sound job-related doesn't mean it can't be turned into a career advantage.

◆ **End-of-Chapter Exercise: Discovering Your Skills**

Most people underestimate their skills—not because they don't have any, but because they've never taken the time to notice them. This exercise will help you identify your hidden strengths, track your progress, and open your eyes to career possibilities you may not have considered before.

Step 1: Start Your Skill Diary

Find a notebook, a notes app on your phone, or a document where you'll keep an ongoing list of things you're good at. This list will grow over time, helping you see your skills evolve and opening up new career ideas down the road.

➤ **Write down at least 15 things you're good at.** Don't just think of big academic skills—add things like organizing, problem-solving, remembering small details, or even knowing how to keep a group conversation going. If something comes naturally to you, it counts.

◆ **Example List:**

- ✔ Explaining things clearly

- ✔ Staying focused on tasks for long periods

- ✔ Noticing when people feel uncomfortable

- ✔ Fixing things when they break

- ✔ Finding the best deals when shopping

- ✔ Writing emails or texts that sound professional

- ✔ Planning vacations or outings

- ✔ Memorizing lyrics, scripts, or information quickly

Step 2: Find Your Hidden Skills

Answer these questions to dig deeper into your strengths:

1 **What are three things people ask you for help with?**
(This could be schoolwork, advice, fixing things, planning events, etc.)

2 **What's something you do without thinking that others struggle with?**
(Are you naturally organized? Do you pick up new skills fast?)

3 **When was the last time you figured something out faster than most people?**
(Maybe you solved a problem, navigated a new situation, or learned something quickly.)

Action Step: Write down your answers in your Skill Diary—these might be skills you hadn't considered before!

Step 3: Career Connection

Now, take **three** of the skills from your list and think of at least **one career** that might use them. If you're stuck, try searching online for careers related to those skills.

📌 **Example:**

✔ **Skill:** You're great at organizing schedules.

  ○ **Possible Careers:** Event planner, logistics manager, executive assistant.

✔ **Skill:** You love helping friends with advice.

  ○ **Possible Careers:** Therapist, human resources, life coach.

✔ **Skill:** You notice when colors don't match.

  ○ **Possible Careers:** Interior designer, graphic designer, fashion stylist.

Step 4: Keep Adding to Your List

Your skills will evolve. What you're good at today isn't the full picture of what you'll be good at in the future.

* Every few weeks, **add something new** to your Skill Diary. Maybe you've gotten better at public speaking, teamwork, or learning new technology.

* If you ever consider a career change, look back at your list. **You might see new opportunities you hadn't thought of before.**

* **What's Next?**

Now that you've identified your skills—**both obvious and hidden**—the next step is figuring out **what you actually enjoy doing.**

In **Chapter 2**, we'll explore your **interests and passions** and how they can shape your career choices. Even if you're good at something, it doesn't mean you love doing it—so let's find the balance.

📖 Chapter 2: What Do You Like?

◆ Why Interests Matter

Being good at something is valuable—but enjoying what you do is just as important.

A lot of people fall into careers simply because they have the skills for them. But if you spend 40+ hours a week doing something you don't enjoy, even a high-paying job can feel miserable.

That's why interests matter when choosing a career. If you like what you do, you'll:

✔ Be more motivated to improve.

✔ Stick with it long enough to build expertise.

✔ Enjoy your daily life instead of just counting down to weekends.

◆ The Reality of Job Satisfaction

Studies have shown that people who feel connected to their work—those who **genuinely enjoy what they do**—report higher overall happiness, productivity, and even better health. On the other hand, **those who work only for a paycheck** often experience burnout, stress, and dissatisfaction.

🖌 **Example:** Two people might have the same job, but their experience can be completely different:

✓ **Person A:** Loves problem-solving and enjoys being a data analyst. They find satisfaction in uncovering insights.

✖ **Person B:** Took a data analyst job because it pays well but finds the work tedious. They constantly think about quitting.

This difference comes down to **interest and engagement.**

☑ Key Takeaway: You don't need to be *obsessed* with your job, but **liking what you do makes a huge difference in long-term success and happiness.**

◆ **Interests Are More Than Just Hobbies**

When people think of "interests," they often limit themselves to hobbies: drawing, playing video games, reading, or working out.

But interests go deeper than that. Think about:

☑ **Environments:** Do you like working in a busy, fast-paced setting or a quiet, structured one?

☑ **Interactions:** Do you enjoy collaborating with people or prefer working independently?

☑ **Tasks:** Are you drawn to creative projects, analytical problem-solving, or hands-on activities?

☑ **Topics:** What subjects do you find yourself reading about or researching for fun?

✦ **Example:** Someone who loves fitness doesn't necessarily need to be a personal trainer. Their interest in **health and wellness** could lead to careers in nutrition, physical therapy, medical research, or even fitness marketing.

☑ **Key Takeaway:** Your interests are more than just "fun activities." They reflect the kind of work you'll enjoy long-term.

◆ Connecting Your Interests to Careers

Some people assume that only **"practical" interests** matter in career planning. But some of the most unexpected interests can turn into careers.

- ✔ **Interest: Psychology & People Behavior** → Possible Careers: Marketing, counseling, human resources, coaching

- ✔ **Interest: Gaming & Strategy** → Possible Careers: UX design, cybersecurity, business strategy, data analysis

- ✔ **Interest: Art & Aesthetics** → Possible Careers: Graphic design, architecture, fashion, photography

- ✔ **Interest: Storytelling & Writing** → Possible Careers: Journalism, content creation, advertising, screenwriting

◆ **Example:** Think about social media influencers. Ten years ago, being a "content creator" wasn't a career path. Now, entire industries exist around video editing, digital branding, and online marketing.

☑ **Key Takeaway:** No interest is "too weird" to be useful—it's all about how you apply it.

◆ End-of-Chapter Exercises: Discovering What You Love

● Step 1: The Interest Exploration Exercise

Reflect on these five key areas to uncover interests you might not have considered.

1 **Childhood Joys** – What activities did you love as a kid? *(Sometimes, forgotten passions reveal career interests.)*

2 **Effortless Engagement** – What tasks make you lose track of time? *(These are things you naturally enjoy doing.)*

3 **Admiration** – Whose careers or achievements do you admire? *(And what about their work appeals to you?)*

4 **Volunteer Ventures** – What causes or issues are you passionate about? *(Helping others, problem-solving, creativity?)*

5 **Learning Curiosity** – What subjects or skills are you eager to learn more about? *(What do you research on your own, just for fun?)*

✓ **Action Step:** Write your answers in your **Skill & Interest Diary** under a new section called **Interests**.

Step 2: The "Perfect Day" Visualization

One of the best ways to figure out what you enjoy is to **imagine a day where everything goes perfectly.**

Instructions:

✔ Find a quiet place, close your eyes, and picture your ideal workday.

✔ Think about:

- What kind of work are you doing?

- Where are you? (An office, a workshop, traveling, at home?)

- Are you working with others or alone?

- What types of tasks are you handling?

- How does the work make you feel?

Example:

- If you imagine working outside, a traditional desk job might not be right for you.

- If you see yourself in a creative environment, a highly structured corporate role might not be the best fit.

Action Step: Write down what you imagined. Even if no clear career pops up yet, **this reveals clues about what makes you happy at work.**

● Step 3: Interest Mapping Exercise

This exercise helps visually connect your interests to potential career paths.

Instructions:

1 **Draw a Circle:** In the center of a blank page, write **"My Interests."**

2 **Branch Out:** Draw lines extending from the center and label each with an interest (e.g., Travel, Technology, Helping Others, Problem-Solving, Design).

3 **Sub-Branches:** Under each interest, list related activities or hobbies you enjoy.

4 **Identify Careers:** Next to each sub-branch, write careers that involve those activities.

✦ **Example:**

- **Interest:** Helping Others → Sub-branch: Teaching → Possible Careers: Teacher, Corporate Trainer, Social Worker

- **Interest:** Creativity → Sub-branch: Graphic Design → Possible Careers: Brand Designer, Web Designer, Digital Illustrator

☑ **Action Step:** Look at your **Interest Map.** Which careers show up multiple times? **Those might be strong matches for you!**

⬤ Step 4: Skill and Interest Alignment

Now, let's combine **what you're good at** with **what you like** to see where they intersect.

Instructions:

1️⃣ Look at your **Skill Diary from Chapter 1**.

2️⃣ Compare it with your **Interest Map from this chapter**.

3️⃣ Draw connections between skills and interests that match.

4️⃣ Research careers that require both those skills and interests.

➡ Example:

✓ **Skill:** You're great at organizing schedules.

✓ **Interest:** You love event planning and social gatherings.

✓ **Career Match:** Event planner, project manager, executive assistant.

☑ **Action Step:** Identify at least **three career paths** that match both your skills and interests.

◆ What's Next?

You now have a better idea of **what excites you and what feels meaningful.** But loving something isn't enough—**you need to find a way to turn that into a sustainable career.**

In **Chapter 3**, we'll look at what **society actually needs and what industries are growing**, so you can find a career that balances **passion, skill, and opportunity.**

📖 Chapter 3:
What Does Society Need?

◆ Why Career Demand Matters

Loving a career and having the skills for it is great—but if no one is hiring for it, or the industry is dying, it won't be sustainable.

Many people make career choices based only on what they like or what they're good at, only to find out later that:

✕ The job market is shrinking.

✕ The pay isn't enough to support their lifestyle.

✕ There's too much competition, making it hard to break in.

To build a career that actually works **long-term**, you need to ask:

☑ **Are there jobs available in this field?**

☑ **Is this industry growing or shrinking?**

☑ **What do employers look for in this career?**

◆ The Importance of Future-Proofing Your Career

✦ **Did you know?** Some jobs that were in high demand 10 years ago **barely exist today**. Think of video rental store clerks, travel agents, and print newspaper editors. **Technology and automation have changed entire industries**, and they will continue to do so.

✔ Example 1: AI is replacing **data entry jobs, telemarketing, and even some legal research roles.**

✓ Example 2: Retail workers are being replaced by **self-checkout machines and online shopping.**

✓ Example 3: Automation in trucking and delivery may replace **millions of driving jobs** in the future.

☑ **Key Takeaway:** It's not enough to pick a career based on today's job market—you need to consider **what careers will still be thriving in 10–20 years.**

◆ **How to Research Career Demand**

Not all jobs offer the same level of growth, stability, and pay. Some industries are booming, while others are shrinking. Here's how to **find the right opportunities:**

1 **Look at Job Growth Trends**

Industries change fast. Some jobs that were in demand 10 years ago barely exist now. Others, like **AI, cybersecurity, and healthcare**, are growing rapidly.

☑ **Where to check job trends:**

✓ **U.S. Bureau of Labor Statistics (BLS)** – Tracks fast-growing jobs.

✓ **LinkedIn & Indeed Job Trends** – Shows hiring demand.

✓ **Industry Reports** – Look at market trends in fields that interest you.

◆ **Example:** The BLS reports that jobs in **renewable energy, cybersecurity, and data science** are among the fastest-growing fields, while **print journalism, manufacturing, and administrative jobs** are on the decline.

2 Check Salary & Job Stability

Some careers pay well but have high burnout (e.g., finance, law).

Others offer stability but low wages (e.g., some social services).

Some jobs require years of training before they pay off (e.g., medicine).

Example Salary Breakdown:

- ✔ **Cybersecurity Analyst** → $100,000+ (high demand, good stability)
- ✔ **Elementary School Teacher** → $60,000 (stable but lower pay)
- ✔ **Journalist** → $45,000 (declining demand)
- ✔ **Physician** → $200,000+ (high pay, but 10+ years of training)

Action Step: Pick **three careers** from your **Interest Map (Chapter 2)** and research:

- Average salary in your region
- Job stability (Is the field growing?)
- Education or experience needed

Hidden Costs of Certain Careers

Some jobs may look good **on paper** but come with unexpected costs:

- ✔ **Doctors and lawyers** make six figures but often start their careers **deep in student loan debt.**
- ✔ **Corporate jobs** may pay well but require **long hours and high stress.**

✔ **Freelancers and entrepreneurs** have **freedom but no guaranteed paycheck.**

☑ **Key Takeaway: Look beyond salary**—consider stress levels, education costs, and work-life balance before committing to a career.

③ Consider Automation & Outsourcing Risks

Technology is replacing some jobs, while others are being outsourced to lower-cost countries.

✔ **Safe Careers:** Healthcare, skilled trades, creative fields, technology development.

✘ **At-Risk Careers:** Data entry, retail, simple bookkeeping.

➤ **Example: Self-driving technology is advancing quickly**—this could impact careers in **trucking, delivery services, and even public transportation.**

☑ **Action Step:** Research if any careers on your list are **at risk of automation or outsourcing.**

◆ The Rise of New & Unexpected Careers

The job market isn't just shrinking in some areas—it's also **creating entirely new careers.**

✔ **Ten years ago, social media managers didn't exist. Now, every company hires them.**

✔ **The demand for virtual reality (VR) developers and AI specialists is growing rapidly.**

✔ **Green energy jobs (like solar panel installers) are booming.**

◆ **Example:** The world is shifting toward **sustainability**—meaning careers in **solar energy, electric vehicles, and environmental policy** will only grow.

☑ **Key Takeaway: The** best career **isn't just one that exists today— it's one that will still be in demand tomorrow.**

◆ **End-of-Chapter Exercise: Testing Career Viability**

● **Step 1: Career Demand Check**

Take your **top three career choices** and research:

✔ Current job openings in your area.

✔ Salary expectations – Can it support your lifestyle?

✔ Growth outlook – Is demand increasing or decreasing?

✔ Skills/education required – Do you have them, or will you need training?

☑ **Write your findings in your Skill & Interest Diary.**

● **Step 2: Industry Trends Research**

Pick **one career field** that interests you and answer:

√ **What's changing in this industry?**

√ **Are new technologies affecting it?**

✓ **Are companies hiring for this role, or is competition too high?**

☑ **Use online sources like:**

- **Google job market reports**
- **Industry news websites**
- **LinkedIn job searches**

☑ **Write a brief summary of what you learn in your Skill Diary.**

⬤ **Step 3: Identifying Transferable Skills**

If a career you're interested in is **shrinking**, can your skills transfer to a related field?

✦ **Example:**

✕ If **print journalism is declining**, a writer might shift to **content marketing, copywriting, or digital media.**

✕ If **traditional retail jobs are disappearing**, someone with sales skills might move into **e-commerce or digital marketing.**

☑ **Action Step:** Write down at least **two alternative career options** that use skills from your top choices.

◆ What's Next?

Now that you've explored what careers are in demand, it's time to **prioritize your skills and interests** to find the strongest career match.

In **Chapter 4**, we'll go through ranking exercises (like MoSCoW) to see **which career paths make the most sense for you.**

📖 Chapter 4:
Choosing a College Major
(Without Stressing About It)

◆ Why Picking a Major Feels So Overwhelming

If you've ever felt pressure to pick the "right" major, you're not alone.

✓ Parents, teachers, and advisors often push students toward **practical** majors.

✓ Society makes it seem like **your major determines your entire life.**

✓ Many students feel stuck between **choosing something they love** and **choosing something that pays well.**

But **here's the truth:**

☞ Your major is **not a life sentence.**

☞ College is **a place to explore, not just train for a job.**

☞ Many **successful people** work in fields **completely different from their degree.**

✅ **Key Takeaway:** College isn't just about getting a degree—**it's about figuring out your strengths, interests, and career possibilities.**

◆ **You Don't Have to Choose a Major Immediately**

Did you know that many colleges **don't require you to declare a major right away?**

✓ Most students **spend their first year taking general education courses.**

✓ You can **explore multiple subjects** before committing.

✓ If you're undecided, **choose a broad major that gives you flexibility.**

◆ **Best Flexible Majors for Undecided Students:**

✓ **Business** – Can lead to marketing, finance, HR, entrepreneurship.

✓ **Communications** – Useful in PR, journalism, advertising, corporate training.

✓ **Psychology** – Opens doors in counseling, HR, market research, education.

✓ **Computer Science** – Leads to coding, cybersecurity, data analysis, AI.

✓ **Liberal Arts** – Great for law, writing, research, nonprofit work.

◆ **Example:**

A student who **likes science but isn't sure about med school** could start with a **biology major** and later specialize in **public health, environmental science, or biotech sales.**

☑ **Action Step:** If you're undecided, **write down three broad majors** that give you room to explore.

◆ **How College Helps You Discover Your Strengths**

Your major isn't the only thing that shapes your career.
College also gives you:

✓ **Internships** – Hands-on experience in different industries.

✓ **Clubs & Extracurriculars** – Leadership, teamwork, and networking skills.

✓ **Study Abroad** – Cultural experience and global career opportunities.

✓ **Networking** – Professors, mentors, and alumni can guide your career.

◆ **Example:**

A student who **majors in psychology** might realize they **don't want to be a therapist**, but they **love understanding human behavior**—which could lead them to **marketing, HR, or user experience (UX) research.**

☑ **Action Step:** Find **one new club, internship, or leadership opportunity that aligns with your interests.**

◆ **How to Flex Your Major into Different Careers**

Even if you pick a major, **you're not locked into one career.** Many degrees are **far more versatile than people realize.**

✦ **Examples of Flexible Degrees:**

> ✔ **English** → Marketing, journalism, PR, corporate training, UX writing
>
> ✔ **Psychology** → Human resources, sales, career coaching, business consulting
>
> ✔ **Biology** → Healthcare management, biotech sales, science communication
>
> ✔ **History** → Law, museum work, policy analysis, research
>
> ✔ **Business** → Finance, entrepreneurship, nonprofit management

✦ **Example:**

A **history major** who doesn't want to be a teacher could **work in law, government, research, or corporate strategy.**

☑ **Action Step:** Research **three career paths** that your major can lead to **outside of the obvious ones.**

◆ **If You Pick the "Wrong" Major, It's Okay**

Many students panic about **choosing the "wrong" major**—but here's why it's not a big deal:

> ✔ You can change majors. Many students do!
>
> ✔ You can add a minor to shift your focus.
>
> ✔ You can pivot after college—many careers don't require specific degrees.
>
> ✔ You can go to grad school in a completely different field.

Example:

A student who **majored in art history** but later became interested in marketing **could pivot into advertising, museum PR, or brand management.**

Action Step: If you're worried about your major, **list three ways to pivot from it if needed.**

◆ **Making the Most of Your Degree (Even If It's Not Perfect)**

Even if you don't love your major, **you can still set yourself up for a great career.**

✔ **Get real-world experience** – Internships, freelance work, or side projects can make your resume stand out.

✔ **Learn in-demand skills** – If your major doesn't teach skills like coding, project management, or social media marketing, take **free online courses** to supplement it.

✔ **Network with professionals** – Your **professors, classmates, and alumni connections** can open doors you never expected.

Example:

A journalism major who realizes **they don't want to be a reporter** could **build skills in copywriting or content marketing** and work in **corporate branding instead.**

☑ **Action Step:** Identify **one skill you can develop outside your major** to increase job opportunities.

◆ **Final Thought: College is Part of the Journey, Not the Destination**

You don't have to have everything **figured out today.**

✔ Your **major is just one piece** of your career puzzle.

✔ College is about **learning, growing, and making connections.**

✔ **The real goal isn't just a degree—it's building a foundation for future success.**

☑ **Key Takeaway:** Your major **matters less** than how you **use it.**

◆ **End-of-Chapter Exercise: Making Smart College Choices**

⬤ **Step 1: List Three Flexible Majors**

✔ Identify **three broad majors** that give you room to explore.

⬤ **Step 2: Research Career Options for Your Major**

✔ Find three careers related to your major outside of the obvious choices.

⬤ **Step 3: Identify One Career-Building Opportunity**

✔ Find **one club, internship, or side project** that can help you gain skills beyond your degree.

☑ **Write your answers in your Skill & Interest Diary!**

◆ **Summary of This Chapter:**

✔ You don't have to pick a major immediately.

✔ College is about exploration—internships, networking, and skill-building matter more.

✔ Most majors are flexible and can lead to multiple career paths.

✔ If you pick the "wrong" major, there are always ways to pivot.

✔ Your major matters less than how you use it.

📖 Chapter 5:
What If You Don't
Want to Go to College?

◆ College Isn't the Only Path to Success

For decades, we've been told that **college is the only way to get a good job**—but that's **not true.**

- ✔ Some of the most **in-demand careers** don't require a degree.

- ✔ Many people **start college without a clear plan** and end up with **debt but no direction.**

- ✔ Some jobs care **more about skills than diplomas**—and there are many ways to gain skills outside of college.

🔲 **Key Takeaway:** If college doesn't feel like the right fit, **you have other options**—and they can lead to just as much success.

◆ **Taking a Gap Year to Figure It Out**

If you're unsure what to do next, you don't have to **rush into a decision.** Many people take a **gap year** to:

✔ Work and gain real-world experience.

✔ Travel and explore different cultures and perspectives.

✔ Try out internships, apprenticeships, or volunteering to see what excites them.

◆ **Example:** A student who isn't sure if they want to work in **healthcare** could **volunteer at a hospital** or **shadow a medical professional** before deciding.

☑ **Action Step:** If you're considering a gap year, **write down three productive ways you could spend it** to help you explore career options.

◆ **Careers That Don't Require a College Degree**

Many **high-paying, stable careers** don't require a four-year degree. Instead, they focus on **skills, training, and certifications.**

◆ **Examples of Great Careers Without a Degree:**

- ✔ **Skilled Trades:** Electrician, Plumber, HVAC Technician, Carpenter

- ✔ **Technology:** Cybersecurity Analyst, Web Developer, IT Support Specialist

- ✔ **Healthcare:** EMT, Dental Hygienist, Medical Coding Specialist, Pharmacy Technician

- ✔ **Creative Careers:** Graphic Designer, Photographer, Video Editor, UX Designer

- ✔ **Business & Marketing:** Real Estate Agent, Sales Representative, Digital Marketing Specialist

◆ **Example:** A student who loves **technology but doesn't want to go to college** could take a **cybersecurity bootcamp** and land a job in IT security.

◆ **Action Step:** Research **three non-degree careers** that interest you and list what skills or certifications they require.

◆ **How to Build Skills Without College**

Some careers require **certifications, trade schools, or bootcamps,** while others value **self-taught skills and portfolios.**

1 Self-Taught & Portfolio-Based Careers

Some industries **care more about skill demonstration** than degrees.

- ✔ **Tech Careers:** Web Development, UX/UI Design, Data Science

- ✔ **Creative Fields:** Graphic Design, Video Editing, Photography

- ✔ **Writing & Marketing:** Copywriting, Content Creation, Social Media Management

How to Get Started Without a Degree:

- ◆ Take free or low-cost courses (**Coursera, Udemy, LinkedIn Learning**).

- ◆ Build a **portfolio** with personal projects or freelance work.

- ◆ Gain experience through **internships, volunteering, or side gigs**.

- ◆ **Example:** Someone who wants to be a **graphic designer** could **teach themselves Adobe Illustrator, create a portfolio, and freelance on Fiverr or Upwork.**

- ☑ **Action Step:** Choose **one skill-based career** and list **three ways to start learning it without college.**

2 Trade Schools & Apprenticeships

Trade schools provide **specialized training** for **high-paying, hands-on careers.**

- ✔ **Shorter than college** (often 6 months to 2 years).

- ✔ **Lower cost** than a four-year degree.

- ✔ **High demand** for skilled tradespeople.

✦ **Popular Trade School Careers:**

✔ Welding

✔ Electrician

✔ HVAC Technician

✔ Auto Mechanic

✔ Commercial Truck Driving

✦ **Example:** An **HVAC technician** can earn **$60K+ per year** after completing a **1-year trade school program.**

☑ **Action Step:** Research **one trade school career** and write down what training it requires.

3️⃣ **Bootcamps & Short-Term Training Programs**

Some careers offer **fast-track training programs** to get you job-ready in **a few months.**

✦ **Examples of Bootcamp Careers:**

✔ **Coding & Tech:** Software Development, Cybersecurity, Data Analytics

✔ **Healthcare:** EMT Certification, Phlebotomy, Medical Billing & Coding

✔ **Business & Marketing:** Digital Marketing, UX/UI Design, Project Management

🔹 **Example:** A coding bootcamp graduate can **land an entry-level job as a web developer** in as little as **4–6 months.**

✅ **Action Step:** Find **one bootcamp program** in a field that interests you and look at its job placement rates.

🔋 **Military Careers & Benefits**

The military offers **job training, education benefits, and career stability.**

- ✔ Paid training in over 150 career fields.
- ✔ GI Bill covers college tuition later if you change your mind.
- ✔ Hands-on experience in leadership, tech, healthcare, and aviation.

🔹 **Example:** Someone who **isn't sure what career they want** but is interested in IT could **join the Air Force or Army in a cybersecurity role** and gain valuable job experience.

✅ **Action Step:** If military service interests you, **research at least two career paths within the military.**

- **Entrepreneurship: Starting Your Own Path**

Some people **don't want to work for someone else**—they'd rather **start their own business.**

- **Examples of Entrepreneurial Careers:**
  - ✔ Freelance Graphic Designer
  - ✔ Social Media Consultant
  - ✔ Personal Trainer
  - ✔ Etsy Shop Owner
  - ✔ YouTuber or Podcaster

How to Get Started Without a Degree:

- Learn business basics (marketing, pricing, client management).
- Offer services on **freelance platforms** (Fiverr, Upwork).
- Test the waters **while working another job.**

- **Example:** A personal trainer could **get certified online, start training clients on the side, and eventually open their own gym.**

- **Action Step:** Brainstorm **one service or product** you could offer as an entrepreneur.

- **Final Thought: Success Has Many Paths**

Whether you go to **college, trade school, bootcamp, or straight into the workforce,** you can still **build a successful career.**

✔ College is one option—not the only option.

✔ What matters is gaining skills, experience, and adaptability.

✔ You can create your own path based on what works for YOU.

☑ **Key Takeaway: Success isn't about the path you take—it's about what you do with it.**

- **End-of-Chapter Exercise: Exploring Non-College Paths**

🔘 **Step 1: Research Three Non-Degree Careers**

✔ Find three careers that don't require a college degree and list their training requirements.

🔘 **Step 2: Identify One Skill to Learn**

✔ Choose **one high-demand skill** you can start learning through self-study, bootcamps, or apprenticeships.

⚫ **Step 3: Explore One Alternative Career Path**

✔ Research **one option** (gap year, trade school, bootcamp, military, or entrepreneurship) and write down the first step to explore it.

☑ **Write your answers in your Skill & Interest Diary!**

◆ **Summary of This Chapter:**

- ✔ College isn't the only path to success.

- ✔ Gap years can help you explore career options before committing.

- ✔ Many careers don't require a degree but do require skills and training.

- ✔ Trade schools, bootcamps, military service, and entrepreneurship are great alternatives.

- ✔ The key to success is gaining skills and experience—no matter how you do it.

◆ **What's Next?**

You now know that **college isn't the only path to success**—but regardless of which path you take, you still need to **prioritize your skills and interests to make the best career choice.**

In **Chapter 6**, we'll go through **how to rank your strengths, interests, and priorities** so you can focus on careers that fit your long-term goals.

📖 Chapter 6: Prioritizing Your Strengths and Interests

◆ **Not Everything Can Be a Priority**

By now, you've identified:

- ✔ What you're good at (Chapter 1)

- ✔ What you like doing (Chapter 2)

- ✔ What society needs and will pay for (Chapter 3)

Now comes the tough part: **prioritizing.**

Not all strengths and interests hold equal weight in career satisfaction. **Some things you love might not be practical as a full-time job.** Some skills you have might not be ones you enjoy using daily.

◆ **The Reality of Compromise in Careers**

A fulfilling career doesn't mean you get **everything you want.** It means balancing three things:

- ✔ **Enjoyment** – You like the work enough to stay engaged.

- ✔ **Competence** – You have the skills or can develop them.

- ✔ **Financial Stability** – The job pays enough to support your lifestyle.

Example:

- **You love music but don't want to be a struggling artist.** Instead of performing, you might consider music production, sound engineering, or marketing for a record label.

- **You're great at math but hate sitting at a desk.** Instead of accounting, you might explore engineering, architecture, or forensic analysis.

- **You love art but need stability.** Graphic design, UI/UX design, or branding could offer creative work with job security.

Key Takeaway: The perfect career doesn't exist—but a great career is one where **you prioritize the things that matter most to you.**

◆ **How to Prioritize Your Strengths and Interests**

A structured way to organize priorities is by using **the MoSCoW Method**.

1 **The MoSCoW Method (Must, Should, Could, Won't Have)**

The MoSCoW Method helps businesses prioritize projects. Here, we'll use it to rank your **strengths, interests, and career needs** by importance.

Instructions: Take your **top 10 skills and interests** and sort them into these categories:

☑ **Must-Have** – Skills/interests that are absolutely essential for career satisfaction.

☑ **Should-Have** – Important but not deal-breakers.

☑ **Could-Have** – Nice to have, but not necessary.

☑ **Won't-Have** – Skills/interests that don't matter as much for career happiness.

◆ **Example:**

✔ **Must-Have:** Creativity, problem-solving, working with people.

✔ **Should-Have:** Writing, leadership, flexible work hours.

✔ **Could-Have:** Travel, social media, graphic design.

✔ **Won't-Have:** Math-heavy work, public speaking, sales.

✅ **Action Step:** Rank your own **strengths and interests** using this method in your **Skill & Interest Diary.**

2 Ranking Your Career Priorities

Some people prioritize **salary and stability**, while others prioritize **passion and flexibility.**

Ask yourself:

- Would I rather make **more money** or have **more work-life balance**?
- Do I want a **stable job** or something that allows **more creativity**?
- How important is **working with people** versus **working independently**?

Now, rank these priorities from **1 to 5 (1 = low importance, 5 = very important):**

- ✔ High Salary 💰
- ✔ Work-Life Balance 🏝️
- ✔ Creativity 🎨
- ✔ Job Stability 📈
- ✔ Opportunities for Growth 🚀
- ✔ Helping Others 🤝
- ✔ Independence 🔍

📌 **Example Prioritization:**

- ✔ **5 (Very Important):** Work-Life Balance, Creativity

✔ **4:** Job Stability, Growth

✔ **3:** Salary

✔ **2:** Helping Others

✔ **1 (Least Important):** Independence

Action Step: Write your rankings in your **Skill & Interest Diary** and reflect on what matters most in your career choice.

◆ **The Dealbreaker Test**

Even if a career matches your **skills and interests**, it might not be the right fit if it clashes with your **non-negotiables**.

Ask yourself:

✔ Do I mind working long hours, or do I need flexibility?

✔ Am I okay with high-pressure jobs, or do I prefer stability?

✔ Do I need a job with clear structure, or do I prefer freedom?

◆ **Example:**

- **A high-stress corporate job may pay well**, but if you hate pressure, it's not a good fit.

- **Freelancing offers flexibility**, but if you need consistent income, it may not work for you.

Action Step: Write down at least **three dealbreakers** you have for a career.

◆ What Happens When You Can't Have It All?

Sometimes, there's a gap between what you want and what's realistic. When that happens, you have **three options**:

- ✓ **Adjust Expectations** – Maybe you love writing but can't make a living as an author yet—so you start with content marketing.

- ✓ **Build Toward Your Dream Job** – If your ideal job requires experience or credentials, you take stepping-stone jobs to get there.

- ✓ **Blend Careers** – You love teaching and technology? Maybe instructional design is a good mix. You love business and creativity? Digital marketing could fit.

◆ **Example:** Someone who wants **to travel, make money, and work independently** might look into **remote consulting, international sales, or travel blogging.**

☑ **Key Takeaway: Career satisfaction comes from balancing reality with what you value most.**

◆ End-of-Chapter Exercise: Creating Your Career Roadmap

Now that you've **prioritized your strengths, interests, and values**, it's time to **create a career plan based on what actually matters to you.**

● Step 1: Write Your Top 5 Career Priorities

Look at your rankings from earlier. Choose your **five most important factors** in a job.

◆ Example:

✔ Work-life balance

✔ Creative freedom

✔ Job stability

✔ Opportunities for growth

✔ Making a difference

☑ Write your top five in your Skill & Interest Diary.

Step 2: List Careers That Align With Your Priorities

Based on what you now know about **your skills, interests, and job market trends**, list at least **three careers** that fit your priorities.

Example Career Matches:

✔ **Top Priority: Creativity + Job Stability** → Careers: UX Designer, Marketing Strategist, Film Editor

✔ **Top Priority: Helping People + Growth** → Careers: Therapist, Human Resources, Health Coach

Write down your top three career matches.

● Step 3: Identify the First Steps Toward Your Top Career Choice

Even if you're not **ready to jump into a new career today,** you can start moving toward it.

- ✔ What skills do you need?

- ✔ Are there online courses or certifications available?

- ✔ Can you gain experience through internships or freelance projects?

◆ Example:

- If you want to become a **UX Designer,** you might start by **taking a free online course in UI/UX design.**

- If you want to be a **career coach,** you might **volunteer to mentor students or new professionals.**

☑ **Write down one small step you can take toward your career goal this month.**

◆ **What's Next?**

Now that you've **narrowed down your career priorities**, it's time to put those ideas to the test. **Before you commit to a career, how do you know if it's the right fit?**

In **Chapter 7**, we'll dive into **internships, job shadowing, freelancing, and other ways to test a career** before going all in.

📖 Chapter 7:
Testing the Waters

◆ **Why You Should "Try Before You Buy"**

You wouldn't buy a car without test-driving it first. So why commit years of your life to a career without experiencing it firsthand?

Many people jump into careers based on **assumptions**—only to realize too late that they don't actually enjoy the work. The best way to avoid that mistake? **Test the waters before committing.**

✅ **Key Takeaway: You don't have to figure everything out right away.** By gaining hands-on experience before fully committing, you can avoid wasting time, energy, and money on a career that doesn't suit you.

◆ **Ways to Test a Career Without a Full Commitment**

1 **Job Shadowing (Best for Seeing the Day-to-Day Reality)**

✔ Spend a **day or week following someone** in the field to see what the job is really like.

✔ Ask professionals in your **network, school, or LinkedIn** if you can shadow them.

✔ Great for careers that sound exciting but **might have hidden challenges** (e.g., long hours, paperwork-heavy roles).

◆ **Example:** You might think being a lawyer is all about dramatic courtroom arguments, but shadowing one might reveal that much of the job involves research, paperwork, and negotiations outside of court.

☑ **Action Step:** Identify **one career you'd like to shadow** and find a professional to contact.

2 Informational Interviews (Best for Insider Knowledge)

✔ A **30-minute conversation** with someone in your desired field.

✔ Helps you **learn about career paths, job realities, and what they wish they knew before starting.**

✔ Reach out via **LinkedIn, alumni networks, or professional groups.**

Example: A nurse might tell you that while they love helping patients, they didn't expect the **long shifts, emotional toll, and high-stress environment** that comes with the job.

Action Step: Make a list of **three professionals** to request an informational interview with.

3 **Internships & Volunteering (Best for Hands-On Experience)**

✔ **Internships (paid or unpaid)** give you a real feel for a job before committing.

✔ **Volunteering can provide valuable experience**, especially in nonprofits or community work.

✔ Great for exploring fields like **education, social work, healthcare, and marketing.**

Example: A student interested in **event planning** might volunteer for a **local nonprofit or festival** to see if they enjoy organizing logistics and managing vendors.

Action Step: Research **internship or volunteer opportunities** related to your career interests.

Freelancing & Side Projects (Best for Testing Independent Work)

✔ If your career idea is **skill-based** (e.g., writing, coding, design), freelancing lets you **test the market before going full-time.**

✔ Websites like **Fiverr, Upwork, and LinkedIn** help you land small jobs to gain experience and confidence.

✔ **Ideal for careers in writing, digital marketing, graphic design, and tech.**

Example: If you think you want to be a **social media manager**, you could start by **running an Instagram or TikTok page for a small business** as a side project.

Action Step: Take on a **small freelance project or personal project** to test your skills.

5 **Online Courses & Certifications (Best for Skill Validation)**

✔ Some careers require specific skills—**taking an online course** can help you determine if it's a good fit.

✔ Platforms like **Coursera, Udemy, and LinkedIn Learning** offer **affordable ways to explore career-related skills.**

✦ **Example:** Someone considering **coding** might take an **intro to Python course** before committing to a full coding bootcamp.

☑ **Action Step:** Find an **intro-level online course** related to a career you're considering.

◆ **The Hidden Benefits of Career Testing**

Even if you test a career and realize it's not for you, **you still gain valuable skills** that transfer to other careers.

◆ **Example:**

- A student **interning at a law office** might decide they don't want to be a lawyer but **realizes they enjoy research**—which could lead to a career in journalism or policy analysis.

- A **volunteer who teaches kids** might not want to be a teacher but **discovers a passion for coaching or training adults.**

✅ **Key Takeaway:** Every experience teaches you something, even if it just **helps you rule out the wrong career.**

◆ **Overcoming Barriers to Career Testing**

Many people hesitate to **test careers** because of fear, time constraints, or financial concerns. Here's how to overcome them:

✕ **"I don't know where to start."**

☑ **Start small.** Ask for an informational interview or take a short online course.

✕ **"I don't have time."**

☑ **Many career tests (like online courses or job shadowing) require just a few hours per week.**

✕ **"I can't afford an unpaid internship."**

☑ **Look for remote, part-time, or paid internships, or volunteer in a way that fits your schedule.**

☑ **Action Step:** Identify **one barrier** holding you back and write down a solution to overcome it.

- **End-of-Chapter Exercise: Putting It Into Action**

● **Step 1: Pick One Career to Explore**

✓ Choose **one career from your shortlist** that you want to test first.

◆ **Example:** If you're interested in UX design, your next step might be taking a **free design course** or reaching out to a UX professional for advice.

☑ **Write down the career you want to test.**

Step 2: Choose a Testing Method

✓ Will you **shadow someone, take an internship, do a freelance project, or interview a professional?**

⚑ **Example:** If you're considering **becoming a therapist,** you might **volunteer at a crisis hotline** or interview a practicing therapist about their experiences.

☑ **Write down your chosen testing method.**

● Step 3: Take One Action This Week

✔ **Send an email,** apply for an internship, or start a project—just take a **small first step!**

✦ **Example Email for an Informational Interview:**

Subject: Exploring a Career in [Field] – Would Love Your Insight

Hi [Professional's Name],

I'm interested in exploring a career in [Field] and would love to hear about your experience. I know your time is valuable, so if you're open to a quick **15-30 minute call,** I'd be grateful for any insights or advice you can share.

Would you be available sometime next week? I'm happy to work around your schedule.

Thanks in advance for your time!

[Your Name]

☑ **Write down the first action you will take this week.**

◆ **What's Next?**

By now, you've learned how to **explore careers before committing—** but what happens when you're ready to take the next step?

In **Chapter 8**, we'll walk through how to **turn career exploration into a real plan**, breaking down your next moves into **manageable, step-by-step actions.**

📖 Chapter 8: Crafting Your Career Action Plan

◆ **Turning Ideas into Action**

You've explored your **skills, identified your interests, researched career demand, prioritized what matters most, and even tested out some options.**

Now, it's time to turn your insights into a **real plan**.

A career doesn't just happen—you have to **build it step by step**. This chapter will help you **create a clear, structured plan** that outlines what you need to do next so you don't feel stuck or overwhelmed.

✅ **Key Takeaway:** A dream career is built through **small, consistent actions**, not one giant decision.

- **Step 1: Set Your Career Goal**

Your goal should be **specific and actionable, not vague** like "I want to be successful."

◆ **Example Goals:**

- ✔ "Get an entry-level job in [career field] within 6 months."

- ✔ "Complete a certification in [skill] by next year."

- ✔ "Land my first freelance project in [industry] within 3 months."

- ✔ "Network with 10 professionals in my industry by the end of this year."

☑ **Action Step:** Write your **career goal** in your **Skill & Interest Diary**.

♦ **Step 2: Do a SWOT Analysis**

A SWOT Analysis (Strengths, Weaknesses, Opportunities, Threats) is a business tool that helps identify potential **challenges and advantages**.

For your chosen career path, ask yourself:

✔ **Strengths (S):** What skills and experiences do I already have?

✔ **Weaknesses (W):** What gaps do I need to fill? (Lack of experience, education, etc.)

✔ **Opportunities (O):** What resources or connections can I use to my advantage?

✔ **Threats (T):** What obstacles could slow me down? (Competition, industry changes, etc.)

📌 **Example SWOT Analysis for an Aspiring Digital Marketer:**

✔ **Strengths:** Strong writing skills, creative thinker, understands social media.

✔ **Weaknesses:** No formal marketing experience.

✔ **Opportunities:** Free online courses, networking events, freelance gigs to gain experience.

✔ **Threats:** High competition, rapidly changing industry.

✅ Action Step: Complete a **SWOT Analysis** for your career path in your **Skill & Interest Diary.**

♦ **Step 3: Set SMART Goals**

SMART goals ensure your action plan is **clear and realistic**.

- **Specific** – Clear and focused ("I will complete an online certification in UX design").

- **Measurable** – Can track progress ("I will complete three modules per month").

- **Achievable** – Realistic ("I can spend 5 hours per week studying").

- **Relevant** – Aligns with your career path ("This certification will help me apply for UX jobs").

- **Time-Bound** – Has a deadline ("I will finish the course in 6 months").

Example SMART Goal:

"I will complete a 6-month online coding bootcamp and build three portfolio projects so I can apply for entry-level developer jobs."

Action Step: Write **one SMART goal** for your career plan.

- **Step 4: Build Your 6-Month Career Action Plan**

Now, break your career goal into **small, manageable steps** to make it less overwhelming.

Example Action Plan (for someone pursuing Digital Marketing):

Month 1:

- Research job descriptions & identify common skills needed.
- Take a free Google Analytics course.

Month 2:

- Start a personal blog or social media project to build experience.
- Connect with 5 professionals in the field on LinkedIn.

Month 3-4:

- Apply for internships or freelance projects.
- Take an SEO or social media marketing certification.

Month 5-6:

- Apply for at least 10 jobs per week.
- Attend an industry networking event.

Action Step: Write a **6-month career action plan** based on your chosen path.

◆ **Step 5: Track Progress & Adjust as Needed**

Your plan isn't set in stone. You might find **new opportunities**, need to **gain more experience**, or shift directions slightly. That's okay!

Ask yourself each month:

- ✔ What progress have I made?
- ✔ What obstacles have I hit?
- ✔ What's my next small step?

◆ **Example:**

- If you planned to get an internship but haven't found one, maybe you **start freelancing instead**.
- If you're struggling with job applications, you **revise your resume or improve interview skills**.

☑ **Action Step:** Set a **reminder to review your progress** every month in your **Skill & Interest Diary**.

◆ **Overcoming Common Roadblocks in Career Planning**

Many people start an action plan but struggle to follow through.
Here's how to tackle common challenges:

✕ **"I don't have enough experience."**

☑ **Solution:** Take free courses, do personal projects, or volunteer to gain skills.

✕ **"I don't have the right connections."**

☑ **Solution:** Start networking on LinkedIn, join industry groups, attend local meetups.

✕ **"I'm afraid of failing."**

☑ **Solution:** Failure is just feedback. Adjust and keep going!

☑ **Action Step:** Identify **one personal roadblock** and write **a solution** for overcoming it.

◆ **End-of-Chapter Exercise: Writing Your Action Plan**

⬤ **Step 1: Write Down Your Career Goal**

   ✔ Make it specific, measurable, and time-bound.

⬤ **Step 2: Complete a SWOT Analysis**

   ✔ List your strengths, weaknesses, opportunities, and threats.

⬤ **Step 3: Break Your Goal into a 6-Month Action Plan**

   ✔ List **small, realistic steps** you can take each month.

☑ **Write your full action plan in your Skill & Interest Diary!**

◆ **What's Next?**

You now have a **clear plan**—but making a plan is only the beginning. **Taking action is where real change happens.**

In **Chapter 9,** we'll cover how to **stay accountable, overcome procrastination, and actually take action on your career goals.**

📖 Chapter 9: Taking Action

◆ Why Action Beats Overthinking

You've done the research, tested career options, and built a solid action plan. Now, it's time for the hardest part: **actually doing it.**

Many people get stuck here. They keep thinking about their plan instead of taking action. They hesitate because they're afraid of making the wrong choice, failing, or not being ready.

But here's the truth: **Nothing happens unless you take the first step.**

☑ **Key Takeaway:** The **perfect** time doesn't exist. **The best time to start is now.**

◆ Step 1: Tackle the First Small Step Today

Instead of looking at the whole journey, just **focus on your first step.**

📌 Example First Steps:

✔ Send an email to request a job shadowing opportunity.

✔ Apply for an internship or freelance gig.

✔ Sign up for a career-related course.

✔ Update your resume and LinkedIn profile.

CAN'T I JUST STAY IN MY ROOM?

✔ Schedule an informational interview with a professional in your field.

✅ **Action Step:** Pick **ONE small action** from your career plan and do it **TODAY.**

◆ **Step 2: Use the Eisenhower Matrix to Prioritize Tasks**

Once you've started, how do you decide what to focus on next? **Use the Eisenhower Matrix to prioritize tasks.**

Sort your tasks into four categories:

1️⃣ **Urgent & Important** – Do these first! (Applying for jobs, preparing for interviews, completing coursework.)

2️⃣ **Important but Not Urgent** – Schedule these. (Building a portfolio, networking, gaining certifications.)

3️⃣ **Urgent but Not Important** – Delegate or streamline. (Resume formatting, organizing files.)

4️⃣ **Not Urgent & Not Important** – Avoid time-wasters. (Over-researching, watching random career advice videos.)

◆ **Example:**

✔ Urgent & Important: Submit three job applications this week.

✔ Important but Not Urgent: Enroll in an online certification course.

✔ Urgent but Not Important: Update LinkedIn profile.

✔ Not Urgent & Not Important: Watching too many motivational career videos.

☑ **Action Step:** Sort your next **five career-related tasks** using the Eisenhower Matrix in your **Skill & Interest Diary.**

◆ **Step 3: Overcome Fear & Self-Doubt**

It's normal to feel nervous or unsure when starting something new. **But fear only wins if you let it stop you from trying.**

How to Get Past Fear:

- ✔ **Afraid of failure?** → Think of failure as learning. Every setback teaches you something useful.

- ✔ **Not feeling "ready"?** → No one is ever 100% ready. Start now, and improve as you go.

- ✔ **Worried about choosing the wrong path?** → You're never locked in. Most people switch careers multiple times.

◆ **Example:** A person who wants to start freelancing might hesitate because they don't feel "expert enough." **Solution:** Take one small project and learn from the experience.

☑ **Action Step:** Write down **one fear or doubt** you have about your career journey. Then, write down **one way to push past it.**

◆ **Step 4: Build Career Habits for Long-Term Success**

Success doesn't happen overnight—it's built through **small, consistent actions.**

Key Habits to Develop:

- ✔ **Daily Career Development** – Spend at least **20 minutes a day** learning, networking, or job searching.

✔ **Networking & Relationship-Building** – Reach out to **one new professional each week.**

✔ **Continuous Skill Growth** – Stay updated with **industry trends, courses, and certifications.**

Example: Instead of waiting for job opportunities, **make a habit of applying for one job per day.**

Action Step: Choose **one career habit** to start this week and track your progress in your **Skill & Interest Diary.**

- **Step 5: Stay Accountable & Motivated**

Taking action is easier when you **hold yourself accountable.**

Ways to Stay Accountable:

- ✔ **Find an accountability partner** – Check in weekly with a friend or mentor about your progress.

- ✔ **Use a progress tracker** – Keep a spreadsheet or journal to record completed steps.

- ✔ **Set mini-deadlines** – If your goal is to build a portfolio, set a deadline for your first project.

- ✔ **Celebrate small wins** – Reward yourself when you hit milestones.

Example:

- ✔ **Goal:** Apply for 20 jobs in a month.

- ✔ **Accountability:** Track progress in a Google Sheet.

- ✔ **Reward:** Treat yourself to a nice dinner when completed.

Action Step: Choose **one accountability method** and write it down.

◆ Handling Setbacks & Rejections

Rejection is a normal part of career growth. Even the most successful people have faced setbacks.

📌 Example:

- ✔ **J.K. Rowling** was rejected by **12 publishers** before Harry Potter was accepted.

- ✔ **Walt Disney** was fired from a newspaper job for "lacking creativity."

How to Handle Setbacks:

- ✔ **Don't take rejection personally.** It's part of the process.

- ✔ **Ask for feedback.** If you get rejected after an interview, ask what you can improve.

- ✔ **Keep going.** The only way to fail is to **stop trying.**

☑ **Action Step:** Write down **one setback you've faced** and how you can learn from it.

◆ **End-of-Chapter Exercise: Taking the First Leap**

● **Step 1: Take One Action Today**

    ✔ Choose **one small, doable task** and complete it.

● **Step 2: Prioritize Your Next Steps**

    ✔ Use the **Eisenhower Matrix** to organize your next **five career-related tasks.**

● **Step 3: Identify & Challenge a Fear**

    ✔ Write down **a fear or doubt** and a **strategy to overcome it.**

● **Step 4: Choose an Accountability Method**

    ✔ Pick a method to **track progress and stay motivated.**

☑ **Write everything in your Skill & Interest Diary!**

◆ **What's Next?**

You're ready to start **building your career**, but what if—somewhere down the line—you **change your mind?**

In **Chapter 10**, we'll explore **how to pivot careers, switch industries, or restart when your career path no longer feels right.**

📖 Chapter 10:
What if You Change Your Mind?

◆ **Your Career is a Journey, Not a Single Choice**

Many people believe that picking a career is a **one-time decision—** but that's not how it works.

The reality is:

✔ **Your interests and skills will evolve over time.**

✔ **New opportunities will appear that you can't predict today.**

✔ **The job market will change, and you'll have to adapt.**

Instead of thinking of your career as a **straight path**, think of it as a **series of opportunities, choices, and pivots**.

☑ **Key Takeaway:** Your **first job** or **first career choice** doesn't define your entire future. **You are always allowed to grow and change.**

◆ **Step 1: Keep Building Skills & Staying Relevant**

The best way to stay **competitive and adaptable** is to **keep learning.**

☑ **Ways to Keep Growing:**

- ✔ Take **courses and certifications** to upgrade your skills.
- ✔ Follow **industry trends** to stay ahead of changes.
- ✔ Attend **conferences, webinars, and networking events.**
- ✔ Read **books, blogs, and listen to podcasts** about your field.

◆ **Example:** If AI is changing your industry, **learn how to integrate AI into your work rather than fearing it.**

☑ **Action Step:** Identify **one skill you want to develop** in the next year and write it in your **Skill & Interest Diary.**

◆ Step 2: Adapt When Life Changes

Your career path won't always go as planned. Maybe you **lose interest**, the industry shifts, or life takes you in a new direction.

◆ Examples of Career Pivots:

- ✔ A **journalist** who shifts into **content marketing** because digital media is growing.

- ✔ A **teacher** who becomes a **corporate trainer** because they want higher pay.

- ✔ An **engineer** who moves into **project management** to lead bigger teams.

The key to staying adaptable is:

- ✔ Being **open to change** instead of resisting it.

- ✔ Looking at how your **skills transfer** to new roles.

- ✔ Keeping your **network strong** so new opportunities come your way.

Action Step: Write down **one way your skills could transfer** to a different career if needed.

◆ Step 3: Set Long-Term Career Checkpoints

Instead of thinking about **one final career goal**, set **career checkpoints** to guide you.

Example Career Checkpoints (5-Year Plan):

☑ **Year 1:** Get entry-level job, internship, or freelance work.

☑ **Year 2-3:** Gain experience, take additional courses, build expertise.

☑ **Year 4-5:** Aim for a promotion, leadership role, or career pivot.

☑ **Action Step:** Create a **5-Year Career Checkpoint Plan** and write it in your **Skill & Interest Diary.**

- **Step 4: Remember That Success is Personal**

Society often defines success in **money, job titles, or degrees.** But real success is **personal.**

Ask yourself:

- ✔ **What does success look like for me?**
- ✔ **What kind of work makes me feel fulfilled?**
- ✔ **How do I want to balance career and personal life?**

Example:

- Some people thrive in **high-powered careers with big salaries.**
- Others prefer **flexibility and work-life balance over money.**
- Some love being **experts in their field,** while others enjoy **switching industries over time.**

Action Step: Write your **own definition of success** in your **Skill & Interest Diary.**

◆ Step 5: Stay Open to Unexpected Opportunities

Sometimes, the best career moves are **the ones you didn't plan for.**

◆ Example:

- A college student working in a **retail job** discovers they love **visual merchandising** and ends up in **fashion marketing.**

- A programmer with a **passion for storytelling** moves into **video game design.**

- A finance major realizes they prefer **helping people** and switches to **financial coaching instead of investment banking.**

☑ **Key Takeaway:** Be willing to **explore, experiment, and embrace opportunities** that come your way.

☑ **Action Step:** Write down a **career opportunity you would have never considered before—but might now.**

◆ **End-of-Chapter Exercise: Future-Proofing Your Career**

● **Step 1: Choose a Skill to Develop**

✔ Identify **one skill** you want to improve in the next year.

● **Step 2: Identify Your Backup Plan**

✔ Write down **one way your skills could transfer** if you ever needed to switch careers.

● **Step 3: Create Your 5-Year Career Checkpoint Plan**

✔ Set **realistic career goals** for the next **5 years.**

● **Step 4: Define Success on Your Own Terms**

✔ Write **what success means for you,** beyond just money or job titles.

☑ **Write everything in your Skill & Interest Diary!**

◆ **What's Next?**

Careers aren't **fixed paths—they evolve.** But how do you make sure that your career stays **relevant, stable, and adaptable to change?**

In **Chapter 11**, we'll talk about **future-proofing your career** so you can **stay ahead of industry shifts, develop skills that never go out of style, and always be prepared for what's next.**

📖 Chapter 11:
How to Future-Proof Your Career

◆ **The Job Market is Always Changing—Are You Ready?**

Imagine choosing a career today and realizing **it doesn't exist in 10 years.**

✔ **Many jobs that existed 20 years ago have disappeared.**

✔ **Technology is evolving faster than ever**, replacing some careers and creating brand-new ones.

✔ **Some industries boom, while others shrink**, making adaptability a crucial career skill.

☑ **Key Takeaway:** The best way to build a stable, successful career is to **stay ahead of changes and keep evolving.**

- **Careers That Have Changed (or Disappeared!)**

- **Examples of Jobs That Have Shrunk:**
  - ✗ Video rental store clerks
  - ✗ Print newspaper journalists
  - ✗ Travel agents
  - ✗ Data entry specialists (AI automation is taking over)

- **Emerging Careers That Didn't Exist 15 Years Ago:**
  - ✔ Social Media Manager
  - ✔ Cybersecurity Analyst
  - ✔ AI & Machine Learning Engineer
  - ✔ UX/UI Designer

- **Example:** Someone who **worked in traditional retail** might need to **pivot into e-commerce or digital customer service.**

- **Action Step:** Research **one industry you're interested in** and look at **how it's evolving.**

- **The Top Career Skills That Will Always Be in Demand**

Some skills **never go out of style, no matter how industries change.**

Skills That Will Keep You Valuable in Any Career:

✔ Critical Thinking & Problem-Solving – AI can process data, but humans solve complex problems.

✔ Communication & Emotional Intelligence – Businesses need leaders, negotiators, and strong communicators.

✔ Tech Adaptability – New tools emerge constantly. Those who can learn new software and AI tools quickly will stay ahead.

✔ Creativity & Innovation – The ability to think outside the box is essential in business, marketing, and technology.

Example: A **graphic designer who learns UX/UI design** stays relevant in **digital product design.**

Action Step: Choose **one skill from this list** and find a way to **strengthen it** (through courses, books, or hands-on projects).

- **How to Become a Lifelong Learner (and Stay Ahead of Industry Changes)**

Instead of focusing on **one specific skill**, focus on **how to learn quickly and efficiently.**

- **Ways to Stay Ahead in Your Industry:**
  - ✔ Take **free online courses** (Coursera, Udemy, LinkedIn Learning).
  - ✔ Follow **industry news and trends** (blogs, podcasts, YouTube).
  - ✔ Join **professional groups or networking events.**
  - ✔ Ask **mentors or colleagues** about new developments in the field.

- **Example:** A marketing professional who **learns SEO and data analytics** becomes more valuable than one who only knows traditional marketing.

- **Action Step:** Write down **one new thing you will learn** in the next **six months.**

◆ The Power of Networking: Build a Safety Net for Your Career

Your **network is your career safety net.** The more **connections** you build, the more **opportunities** you'll find.

◆ How to Build & Maintain a Strong Network:

- ✔ Stay connected with colleagues, mentors, and classmates.
- ✔ Follow industry leaders on LinkedIn and engage with their content.
- ✔ Join professional organizations related to your career field.
- ✔ Be willing to help others—networking is a two-way street.

◆ **Example:** A former teacher who wants to shift into **corporate training** can start **connecting with professionals in HR and learning development.**

☑ **Action Step:** Identify **one networking opportunity** you can take this month.

◆ **How to Stay Employable in a Rapidly Changing Job Market**

    ✔ Keep an eye on **emerging trends** in your field.

    ✔ Be willing to **take risks and try new things.**

    ✔ Regularly **update your resume, skills, and online presence.**

📌 **Example:** A **journalist who adapts to digital media trends** (SEO, content marketing) **stays employable** in a changing industry.

☑ **Action Step:** Find a **trend in your field** and write down **one way to prepare for it.**

- **The 3-Year Career Check-In: Are You Still Growing?**

To **stay relevant and avoid getting stuck**, check in on your career **every three years.**

- **Ask Yourself:**

  - ✔ Am I still learning and growing?

  - ✔ Has my field changed? Am I keeping up with new trends?

  - ✔ Am I happy in my role, or do I need a change?

- **Example:** If you're in an **IT role that's becoming automated**, it might be time to **learn AI-related skills or project management.**

- **Action Step:** Set a **calendar reminder for a career check-in** every three years.

◆ **End-of-Chapter Exercise: Planning for the Future**

● **Step 1: Choose a Skill to Develop**

    ✔ Identify **one skill** you want to improve in the next year.

● **Step 2: Identify a Trend in Your Industry**

    ✔ Find **one career trend** that's growing and list a way to prepare for it.

● **Step 3: Take One Action to Future-Proof Your Career**

    ✔ Choose **one action** (networking, taking a course, testing a new tool) that will help you stay ahead.

☑ **Write your answers in your Skill & Interest Diary!**

◆ **Final Thought: The Future is Yours to Shape**

✔ Your career is a journey, not a fixed path.

✔ Industries will change—but you can change with them.

✔ The more adaptable, skilled, and connected you are, the more opportunities you'll have.

☑ **Key Takeaway: The best way to secure your future is to keep learning, growing, and staying adaptable.**

- **Summary of This Chapter:**

  ✔ The job market constantly evolves—stay ahead of it.

  ✔ Certain skills (problem-solving, communication, adaptability) will always be valuable.

  ✔ Lifelong learning keeps you competitive—embrace new skills and technologies.

  ✔ Networking helps you find opportunities before you need them.

  ✔ Checking in on your career every 3 years helps you stay on track.

- **Final Thought: Your Career is Yours to Shape**

This book has given you the tools to **find your career path, test it, plan for it, and take action.**

But remember:

  ✔ **No decision is permanent.** You can pivot and adapt.

  ✔ **Learning never stops**—keep growing.

  ✔ **You define success, not anyone else.**

You're in control of your future. Go out there and **build it.**

- **What's Next?**

Now you know how to **stay ahead in a changing job market, develop long-term skills, and build a strong career foundation.**

So what's left? **Taking control of your future.**

In **Chapter 12 (Conclusion),** we'll wrap everything up and leave you with a final **push to take action and shape your own career path.**

📖 Chapter 12: Conclusion (Your Future is in Your Hands)

◆ **You've Done the Hard Work—Now It's Time to Move Forward**

You started this journey with a big question:

"What should I do with my life?"

Now, you have a **roadmap** to help you figure it out.

✓ You've **identified your skills and strengths.**

✓ You've **explored what excites you.**

✓ You've **researched career demand and opportunities.**

✓ You've **learned how to pivot if you change your mind.**

✓ You've **discovered ways to future-proof your career.**

✓ You've **created a plan, tested options, and taken action.**

That means you're already **ahead of most people.**

But here's the real secret: **Your career is just getting started.**

◆ **Your Career is Not Set in Stone—And That's a Good Thing**

If there's **one thing** you take away from this book, it should be this:

Your career is a **journey, not a final destination.**

✓ **It's okay to change your mind.** What you want today may evolve in five or ten years.

✓ **It's okay to take an alternative path.** College isn't the only route to success.

✓ **It's okay to pivot when industries change.** The best careers grow with you.

☑ **Key Takeaway:** You are never "stuck." You can **always** learn, pivot, and create new opportunities for yourself.

◆ **Future-Proofing Your Career Starts Now**

The world **will keep evolving.** Some jobs will disappear, new careers will emerge, and industries will shift.

The best way to prepare?

✓ **Stay adaptable** – Keep learning new skills and exploring opportunities.

✓ **Build relationships** – Your network can open doors you never expected.

✓ **Think long-term** – The best careers grow and evolve with you.

◆ **Example:**

If a career in **marketing or design** shifts more toward **AI and automation**, staying **ahead of digital trends** will help you stay relevant.

☑ **Action Step:** Write down **one skill you'll focus on improving** in the next year to keep yourself future-proof.

- **What Happens Next? You Decide.**

This book has given you the **tools** to figure out your path.

But **what you do next is up to you.**

- **You can take small steps today**—send an email, apply for a job, start a project.

- **You can commit to growing your skills**—take a course, find a mentor, push yourself.

- **You can redefine success on your terms**—build a career that fits **YOU**, not someone else's expectations.

The **only** wrong choice? **Doing nothing.**

- **Action Step:** Write down **one career action you will take in the next 24 hours.**

◆ **Final Thought: Your Career is Yours to Shape**

If you ever feel lost again, **come back to this process:**

✓ Look at your **skills.**

✓ Check in with your **interests.**

✓ See what's happening in the **job market.**

✓ **Test new opportunities.**

✓ **Make a plan and take action.**

Your career is **yours to create**—one step at a time.

Now **go make it happen.** 🚀

About the Author

Jennifer Larsen has a habit of turning big questions into clear, doable steps—and she's built a career around helping others do the same. With a background in education and psychology (and a low tolerance for boring advice), she has created this guide for anyone tired of being asked, "What do you want to be when you grow up?"—especially if they're already grown.

www.ingramcontent.com/pod-product-compliance
Lightning Source LLC
Chambersburg PA
CBHW051430090426
42737CB00014B/2902